Productivity

Overcome Procrastination &
Achieve More in Less Time

Rowan Marshall

©Copyright 2021 by Cascade Publishing

All rights reserved.

It is not legal to reproduce, duplicate, or transmit any part of this document in either electronic means or in printed format. Recording of this publication is strictly prohibited.

Table of Contents

Introduction 1
Chapter 1: Making Productivity Work For You 4
    Self-Discipline Makes Productivity Easier 4
    How To Improve Your Self-Discipline 6
    Overcoming Procrastination To Drive Productivity 10
    The Vicious Cycle Of Procrastination Reduces Productivity 13
Chapter 2: Building Healthy Habits That Promote Productivity 15
    Lifestyle Habit Changes That Improve Productivity 16
Chapter 3: Keeping Your Mind Clear 25
    Using Mindfulness To Keep You Focused In The Present 25
    Mindfulness Meditation Guide 28
    Starting Your Tasks 31
Chapter 4: Productivity Strategies 34
    Removing Your Distractions And Temptations 34
    Reward System 36
    The Pomodoro Technique 36
    Two-Minute Rule & Motivation 38
    Time Blocking 40
    Play A Game Using Your To-Do List 41
    Goal Setting 41
    Outsourcing Tasks 42
    The 80-20 Rule 42
    Parkinson's Law 43
Conclusion 45

Introduction

Productivity can be the difference between taking one hour to complete a task, or taking five hours to complete that exact same task. Increasing productivity is encouraged to anybody, regardless of the reason, it should always be welcomed with open arms. An athlete can boost productivity to make their workouts more efficient, and as a result increase their strength, speed, or endurance. An entrepreneur will benefit from improving their productivity to grow and scale their business to new heights. Irrespective of what you may require productivity for, the recipe remains the same.

Productivity is a direct combination of self-discipline and your ability to overcome procrastination. Self-discipline is one of the most useful skills you can wield. It is a skill that benefits every aspect of your life. Although many people understand the importance of this skill, not many take the time and effort to improve their discipline. A common myth regarding self-discipline is that those who practice it are always living in a strict and limited lifestyle. On the contrary, self-discipline merely means having better self-control and increasing one's inner strength to control themselves, their behavior, and reactions.

One of the main traits of self-discipline is denying instant gratification and pleasure in return for a more significant gain, which requires you to put in the effort and time to achieve. Most people know that self-discipline is one of the most crucial components when it comes to success but fail when it comes time to put in the work. You may notice that a lot of self-disciplined individuals don't fear failure, they thrive in the face of adversity and push through, they stick to routines/plans/diets/etc. and hold themselves accountable no matter the cost.

The second part of the recipe for productivity is overcoming procrastination. Procrastination is so widely common that whole industries such as self-help are valued at over 9 billion dollars! Full of programs, books, and material to help people overcome this frustrating habit. Procrastination is a challenge that everyone faces at some point in their lives. For as long as the human race has existed, people have struggled to avoid, delay, and procrastinate on simple tasks, and even ones that matter most to them.

In our most productive flashes, the moments where we have temporarily figured out how to overcome procrastination, we often feel accomplished and satisfied. Worry less; you are not alone in the pursuit of achieving high productivity. This setback is so well-documented and undying that ancient Greek philosophers like Aristotle and Socrates created a word to depict procrastination: Akrasia. Akrasia means the 'state of acting against your better judgment.' It translates to 'when a person is doing something, although they know that they ought to be doing something else.' A loose paraphrase of this is that akrasia is simply a lack of self-control. Today's modern definition of procrastination is 'the act of delaying or postponing a task or set of tasks.' Ultimately, whether you refer to procrastination as procrastination or akrasia, or maybe even something else, it all leads to the same meaning, which is the 'force' that is preventing you from doing the things that you had set yourself up to do.

You can drive productivity much higher by accomplishing better self-discipline and reducing procrastination. Moreover, by implementing healthier habits that help with the two ingredients in this recipe, you will begin to automate certain behaviors and tasks to make create a rippling effect. The chapters within this book will help you better understand the science behind this and what you need to do to accomplish higher productivity.

Chapter 1:

Making Productivity Work For You

Productivity is a healthy balance between utilizing a strong sense self-discipline to complete essential tasks and overcoming urges of procrastination. Understanding how to increase your self-discipline while overcoming your destructive habits will help you maximize your productivity. Learn how to overcome procrastination by identifying common excuses that are used to procrastinate and how to avoid the vicious cycle of procrastination.

Self-Discipline Makes Productivity Easier

Understanding the psychology behind self-discipline is exceptionally important as it will help you learn what the driving factors are behind it. One of the main factors that drive self-discipline is willpower. Surprisingly, a lot of people believe they could change their lives for the better if they were instilled with more willpower. If everyone applied more willpower, they would save responsibly for retirement, exercise regularly, stop procrastinating, increase productivity, and achieve all of their noble goals. One survey that studied the annual stress of Americans found that most participants reported lacking willpower as the number one reason for not achieving the goals they set for themselves.

The study uncovered that the biggest obstacle for anyone wishing to achieve change was a lack of willpower. Even though many people often blame the scarcity of their willpower for their unhealthy choices, they are still grasping on to the hope of achieving it one day. The majority in this study also reported that they think willpower can be taught and learned. And they are correct! There are numerous techniques that we can implement to strengthen our willpower with some training and practice.

Weak self-discipline isn't the only reason for someone to fail at achieving their goals. Psychologists in the field of willpower have built three critical components when it comes to achieving goals. First, it is said that you need to set a clear goal and then establish the motivation for change. The second component was to monitor your behavior in regards to that goal. Willpower itself is the third and final component. If your goal is similar to the following; stop smoking, get fit, study more, or stop wasting time on the internet, willpower is a critical concept to understand if you are looking to achieve any of those goals.

The bottom line of willpower is resisting temporary temptations and urges to achieve long-term goals. Here are several reasons why this is beneficial. Over a regular school year, psychologists performed a study that examined the self-control in a class of eighth-grade students. The researchers in this study did an initial assessment of the students' self-discipline by asking them, their parents, and teachers to fill out a questionnaire. They took it one step further and offered these students the option of deciding whether they want to receive $1 right in this moment, or $2 if they waited just a single week. At the end of the study, the results highlighted that the students who held superior test scores, better school attendance, higher grades, and participated in competitive high school programs, all ranked high on the self-discipline assessment. These researchers found that self-discipline played a more prominent role than IQ when predicting academic success. Additional studies have resulted in similar conclusions.

In another study, researchers queried a group of undergraduate university students to fill out self-discipline questionnaires that they used to assess the students' self-control. These researchers developed a scale that helped score the students on the strength of their willpower. The study found that the students with more self-esteem, improved relationship skills, a higher GPA, and less alcohol or drug abuse all had the highest self-control scores.

How To Improve Your Self-Discipline

Many things can be done to learn self-discipline and tap into your will power source to start becoming more productive. Below is a 10-step guide for you to follow. This guide is a fool-proof way to start improving your self-discipline to drive higher productivity.

1. Identify your weaknesses.

Everyone has their own set of weaknesses and temptations. They may range from a specific type of food like chocolate, a social media platform like Instagram, or even a newly released video game. Regardless of what the temptation may be, the effect has comparably damaging results for everyone.

The first step to mastering your self-discipline is acknowledging your shortcomings, no matter what they might be. People often try to disguise their weaknesses, or pretend they don't exist to portray themselves as strong individuals. This avoidance is exceptionally ineffective in relation to enhancing your self-discipline. The purpose of acknowledging your weaknesses is not to make yourself feel bad; instead, it helps you recognize your weak points, and help you plan out how to overcome them. Acknowledge your flaws; it is impossible to overcome them until you do.

2. Remove your top temptations.

Once you have accepted your weaknesses, you can now move on to step two, remove your temptations. Like we mentioned in step one, everyone has their own set of flaws, and it can range from small urges like an unhealthy snack to something more drastic that hinders your productivity, like playing a video game for hours on end. By understanding your faults, you can make accommodations for yourself that will help eliminate some of those temptations.

3. Set specific goals and write an execution plan.

To continue strengthening your self-discipline, you must have a clear vision of what goals you are trying to accomplish. It is important to also have an understanding of what success really means. If you don't know where you're planning to go or what achieving your goals even entails, it is easy for you to lose your way or become sidetracked.

Make sure the goals that you are setting have a clear and concise purpose. For example, don't use goals like "I want to be rich within the next five years." This goal is too broad for it to have a convincing significance. Instead, you should construct a goal that is quantifiable like "I am planning on saving $20,000 by the end of this year." Subsequently, you now have a measurable goal, and you can create a strategy that makes sense to you. To dive deeper into this, you can break down these goals even further and figure out where you can save money, or how you can make even more money on the side.

4. Start practicing your self-discipline by actually using it.

The more time you spend practicing self-discipline, the more difficult it can become to keep utilizing your willpower. Sometimes when a person faces a big temptation or decision, they may feel that overcoming that considerable temptation makes it harder for them to continue to overcome other tasks requiring self-discipline. The only way to move past this is to have the right mentality and a good set of goals prepared. By having a good mindset, it creates a buffer for how quickly your willpower becomes drained. Preparation is also crucial, understanding what is to come next helps you mentally prepare before it actually happens, limiting any possible surprises or temptations.

5. Build new and healthy habits.

To strengthen your self-discipline, you need to instill new habits, which can immediately feel very intimidating, especially if you concentrate all of your focus on the end goal. To avoid this daunting feeling, keep any changes very simple. Break your bigger goals into smaller achievable habits. Instead of trying to accomplish one colossal goal all at once, or alter all of your destructive habits, simply focus on undertaking just one habit consistently, and exercise your self-discipline with that one small task. Once you feel comfortable with that new habit, try adding in something new. Remember at any time if you become overwhelmed, there is nothing wrong with taking a step back and revisiting those extra habits at a later time.

6. Incorporate a healthy diet.

Did you know that glucose levels play a significant role in the human brain? The sensation of being hungry can cause people to feel angry, annoyed, and irritated. This feeling is real, and everyone has experienced it before, possibly weakening their willpower. Research has found evidence that having low blood sugar weakens a person's ability to make good decisions.

When you are hungry, your ability to concentrate suffers greatly, and your brain won't function to an optimal level. Therefore, your self-control is likely to be weakened in this state. To prevent this, make sure to be eating several smaller meals to prevent yourself from feeling that annoying feeling of hunger, that may cause you to have a lapse in judgment. Since exercising willpower takes up a lot of energy from the human brain, make sure to keep fueling it with enough glucose so that the brain can keep functioning at its peak.

7. Adjust your beliefs regarding willpower.

An individual's internal perception about willpower and self-control plays a huge role in determining how much willpower they cultivate. If a person can remove these obstacles by believing that they have a large stockpile of willpower and believing in themselves, they are less likely to drain out their willpower than someone who believes that they hold a limited supply. So try changing your perception of how you see your willpower. Try to think of it as a source that can still run out, but you have a larger stockpile in storage.

8. Always devise a backup plan.

Many psychologists use a well-known technique that helps with boosting willpower called "implementation intention." This technique is where you generate a plan to follow when you face a potentially difficult situation. By strategizing before entering into this testing situation with destructive temptations, you will have an action plan in place where you can instinctively turn to, rather than have to come up with an excuse or idea on the spot and risking failure. Upon entering these situations with an action plan, you allow yourself a stronger mindset and in turn, more self-control to overcome obstacles that may stand in your way. You will save a lot of energy by not having to make sudden decisions or make sudden plans based on your emotional state in the current moment. This energy-saving will make you less likely to cave in to temptations and more likely to exercise your self-discipline.

9. Reward yourself frequently.

Like anything in life, it is necessary to give yourself a break and reward yourself from time to time. Gift yourself something to look forward to by planning an appropriate reward upon accomplishing your goals. This concept is not much different from when you were a little kid, and you received a treat from your parents for demonstrating good behavior. When you have something to look forward to, it gives you extra motivation needed to succeed.

10. Forgive your failures and keep progressing.

Even with all the best intentions and the most thought-out plans, sometimes they may fall short. Avoiding failure altogether is impossible, and we should not build a mindset around that ideology. Everyone will have their ups and downs, their successes, and their failures. The key to overcoming the failures that you will face is simply to keep moving forward. If you stumble on your journey of self-discipline, instead of giving up altogether, acknowledge what caused it, learn from it, and then move on. Don't let yourself get caught up in frustration, anger, or guilt because these emotions are the ones that will de-motivate you and get in the way of your future progress.

Overcoming Procrastination To Drive Productivity

In the world we live in today, where distractions are plentiful, procrastination is becoming the number one adversary to productivity. Understanding the excuses that are commonly used to encourage procrastination will assist in redirecting your focus back on track. Let's learn about what the most common excuses are and how the process of procrastination works.

1. "I will do it tomorrow."

An old saying goes, "never put off till tomorrow what you can do today." Unfortunately, this saying does not stand up well in the face of temptation or instant gratification. Instead of resisting temptation, try to think of it in a way where you're doing yourself a favor. Promise yourself some type of reward (e.g., getting your favorite takeout or drawing yourself a nice bath) if you complete that required task today instead of 'tomorrow.'

2. "I don't have time to do this right now."

The people who rely on this excuse the most are generally busy professionals. If you're frequently on the go and completing tasks but still never getting to the end of your to-do list, it may feel natural to think that you don't have time for whatever task you promised yourself you would do. However, there is a huge flaw in this mentality. It is all about priorities. There will always be time to work on something; you just have to make room for it.

3. "This is too difficult to do right now; I'll do it later."

Individuals that set themselves up for large tasks without creating a plan often fall victim to this excuse. When you look at a huge set of tasks, all you can see is how big and overwhelming that one entity is. When all you're thinking about is how big that workload is, it's almost expected that you would want to avoid it for as long as possible. Rather than looking at your one large task as a monstrous unit, break it down into smaller chunks. Breaking down your task into smaller objectives and focusing on those smaller duties individually will feel far less intimidating.

4. "I will start working on task B once I've finished task A."

When you have two competing tasks or goals, inevitably, one is going to take a backseat for the time being. While it can be advantageous to have more than one priority, dividing your attention is not ideal for confronting multiple tasks. For instance, let's say that you are working on two projects with the same deadline at the end of the week. By the end of your first day working, you've already made a considerable impact on project A, but you don't want to start project B because you don't want to shift gears. Understand that it is absolutely ok to shift gears before the completion of one task is complete. There may be some downtime, this could be a perfect time to switch it up and prepare task B and speed up your workload. Remember progress is progress, as long as you're focused on your tasks at hand, all will be well.

5. "This task is really important; it needs my full attention."

The most common victims to this excuse are your nervous professionals. For instance, let's pretend that you have neglected a huge project for a quite some time now, but there are a ton of your daily tasks that you still need to complete. If you truly believe that your project is the most important thing right now, you may decide to do it at a time when you aren't so distracted by other trivial tasks. You will always run into interferences, and there is no 'perfect' time to do something. Rather than saying now is not the best time to work on it, break it down into smaller tasks and just do one of them amidst your other tasks.

6. "I'm too tired right now to do this (or stressed, angry, sad…)"

This excuse is probably the most common, and tempting excuse of them all. If you find yourself in a negative mood, all you want to do is stop working and do something that will make yourself feel better. This could include just sitting at home relaxing or going out for a beer. You may then begin rationalizing that you would finish your work faster and be more productive if you tried to attempt it later when you're feeling more up to it. There are two important aspects to note here. First of all, it is impossible to tell what kind of mood you will be in the future. For all we know, you could be in the same mood tomorrow and fall into the same excuse in some sort of unproductive loop. Secondly, this is not a common thought, but working through a hard task can actually enhance your mood. The feeling of achievement and satisfaction that comes with finishing a task, no matter how pleasant or unpleasant, can often lift you out of a bad mood. Especially if you gift yourself with a reward after accomplishing what you set out to do.

The Vicious Cycle Of Procrastination Reduces Productivity

Procrastination arises from some of our own unhelpful rules and assumptions that we have of ourselves and the rest of the world. When these rules and assumptions are activated, they lead you to detect some sort of discomfort about undertaking a task or job that you've set up for yourself in the past. If you are unable to tolerate this discomfort, you will likely utilize procrastination to avoid this discomfort. More often than not, you will come up with pretty convincing justifications or excuses for different forms of procrastination. Thus, you will engage in activities in search of instant gratification that create a pleasurable distraction as a substitute for the intended task. In return, some consequences come up due to this procrastination, which will make you more likely to go down the route of further procrastination the next time you face a similar task or duty. This cycle occurs because you received a 'reward' or pay-off for your procrastination, and you have subsequently made that task even more aversive by avoiding it in the first place.

Here is a little chart that will help explain it further to help visualize this cycle.

Approach Task/Goal

Unhelpful Rules and Assumptions Are Activated
- Pleasure seeking, fear of failure or disapproval, need to be in charge, fear of uncertainty or catastrophe, low self-confidence, depleted energy

Discomfort Driven
Detect discomfort from the task or goal, disliking the feeling of discomfort, the urge to avoid the discomfort increases + Procrastination Excuses

Procrastination Activities
Search for instant gratification

Consequences

Continue to Procrastinate Next Time

Chapter 2:

Building Healthy Habits That Promote Productivity

Our daily routine, including the way we work, relax, and have fun, are all built upon our habits. Now, let's learn a little about how humans develop habits. Why is it that when most people try to break their habits and change them for the better, they can only seem to stick with it for a certain amount of time before returning to their old ways and giving up entirely? The answer is that the human brain requires repetition to build habits over numerous months, years and decades. Habits are the neural pathways that the brain has solidified over time. This pathway formation happens on a biological level. These neural pathways are responsible for linking up the neural networks in the human brain to perform a specific function like brewing a coffee in a specific way, walking up the stairs, or smoking a cigarette.

The neural pathways in the human brain help us to automate specific actions and behaviors that we often perform to reduce the conscious processing power of the brain. This allows the mind to focus on alternative functions rather than the habitual tasks it has rehearsed repeatedly a thousand times. This ability developed early on in the evolution of the human species and is embedded into our DNA; it enables the human race to a more efficient cognizance that they can divert toward more critical thoughts.

Typically, it's the routine behaviors that we repeatedly perform every day that hold us back from developing healthy habits. Over time you may have cultivated an abundance of damaging habits, which add negative value to your life as opposed to the good habits that further drive you to achieve your goals and aspirations. Since your neural pathways entrench themselves deeper and deeper over time, it becomes harder to break bad habits and begin to nurture healthier behaviors with all of the pre-existing harmful habits relentlessly getting in the way. However, if you can attempt to grasp the next few following habits we will be discussing into your life, you will find that strengthening your productivity may become a lot easier.

Lifestyle Habit Changes That Improve Productivity

Let's now look at a few different habits that will help to increase your productivity levels and improve your self-discipline simultaneously.

1. Practice gratitude frequently.

A huge problem in our modern world today is that we constantly distract ourselves with millions of sophisticated items, thoughts, experiences, etc., that cause us to always be wanting something more or something else. This distraction causes us to devote too much time into thinking about all the things we want. Building a habit of expressing gratitude prevents us from always desiring the things we don't have and moving forward towards appreciating and being content with the things we do have. When you express appreciation, you can begin to make remarkable changes in your life.

The effects of practicing and showcasing gratitude are extremely beneficial. Supporting everything from improved mental health, emotional well-being, spirituality, gratitude is capable of so many extraordinary effects. Practicing gratitude is an exercise that is incessantly implemented in therapy to help the client move away from negative judgements and encourage mindfulness and positivity. Gratitude helps us move towards a state of abundance and away from a sense of deficiency. When you get stuck in a state of lack, it becomes difficult to focus on realizing your goals and inviting productivity. Avoid expending too much mental capacity and energy worrying about things that hold no value, or living fearfully to the point that you forget about the things you already have.

Unfortunately for some, this state of lack can also mature into more evident physical symptoms. One indication is stress, in which the brain will instinctively release cortisol and epinephrine, which are the stress hormones from our brains. These hormones impact numerous systems within the human body. When you become stressed, your immune system, digestive system, and reproductive system are all affected. Encouraging a few moments every single day writing down everything that we are grateful for can be a great exercise. Yes, there may be times where you feel like you don't have anything to be grateful for, dig deep and consider that sometimes being grateful for simple things such as your health is more than enough. It could be something very simple like the delightful weather, the brief but polite conversation you had with your barista, or even just seeing that cute dog on your way home.

2. Forgiveness.

If you live a fast-paced life, how often do you find yourself feeling angry, frustrated, or annoyed? Due to the insane amount of convenience we grow accustomed to in our day to day lives, simple irritations occurring throughout our day can cause a spiral of negative emotions. Imagine this, you are in a rush to get to work and you happen to be running late that day. The coffee shop that you normally stop to get your morning coffee is taking forever to complete your order. When you finally get your coffee, you realize that the barista had made your order wrong, but of course you don't have the time to fix the order. That one simple human error has propelled you into a spiral of frustration and annoyance. You struggle to let go it go, and later discover that it had negatively impacted your entire day. This mentality triggers you to consume a lot of your energy source upset about this one minor mishap. You'll find that you don't have enough mental capacity to focus on other tasks like practicing your self-discipline to improve productivity. When you spend most of your days feeling guilt, anger, or regret, you are cultivating more issues than you are resolutions. The emotions of anger and hate consume much more energy within your body than positive emotions like forgiveness and love. The best thing is, forgiveness is something that you can learn. And when you learn to forgive, you will be able to let things go, and move forward.

Without forgiveness, you will simply struggle to maintain high levels of productivity. If you are too worried about how someone or something has wronged you, it makes it nearly impossible for you to focus on achieving your goals, or on upholding your discipline. If someone has hurt you in the past, try to learn forgiveness enough to forgive them. Doing this doesn't mean that you have to forget about what they did to you altogether. Simply just forgive and let go of that negative energy and release it back to the universe, rather than keeping that negativity stored within your body. When we perform the act of forgiveness, we are letting go of the negative energy that inhibits our ability to practice high productivity. If you want to maximize your productivity, you have to get rid of sources sucking away at your mental energy. Holding on to negative emotions like anger is a sure way for your energy to drain. While forgiveness might not seem like a habit that drives productivity at first glance, it is an extremely crucial practice to improve on.

3. Mindfulness and meditation.

Just like gratitude, meditation is a commonly used technique to help people practice mindfulness when suffering from anxiety, stress or depression. Meditation is a great exercise to help put your mind at ease, and provide you with balance in the form of spirituality that you may use as a means for growth. When you practice meditation, you drift your awareness away from things of the past and future and concentrate it toward the present moment in time. The ability to stay mindful greatly increases your ability to stay focused on one present task, preventing your mind from wandering off to potential distractions.

4. Active goal setting.

Setting small but attainable goals is far more effective than setting broad and larger goals. Setting smaller goals becomes more quantifiable, and because of this, you can easily keep track of your progress when it comes to goal achievement and evaluation. Keeping track of your completed goals and uncompleted goals is a fool-proof way of identifying how productive you are being and thus, allowing you to alter your working habits and strategies as required.

Passive goal setting and active goal setting are significantly different strategies. Passive goal setting involves only setting goals without planning or detail into how this goal will be reached. Passive goal setting doesn't really define the actual goal, making it hard for you to keep track of your progress and know what you need to do to achieve that goal along the way. Active goal setting is the complete opposite of passive goal setting. Active goal setting involves writing out goals and linking them to an action. These goals have to be measurable and very specific. To successfully form an active goal, you must define a plan towards achieving it. For this reason, your long-term goals are broken down and engaged in smaller goals daily.

Implementing active goal-setting instills the discipline needed deep within you because you lay down a direction. By breaking down your big goals into smaller daily objectives you avoid distractions by narrowing your focus toward what you need to get done in the present day. This way, you're not left constantly thinking about one large intimidating goal and not knowing how to approach it.

If you have long-term goals like; wanting to own your first home, wanting to pay off your student debt in the next three years, or taking six months off to travel Europe, you need to actively participate in daily, weekly, and monthly goal setting and planning. You have to play an active role in tracking your progress toward your goals, and make revisions in areas where you feel like aren't working in your favor.

So take out a pen and a piece of paper, and start writing down any long-term goals you may have. Once you have some long-term goals written down, break it down into monthly, weekly, and daily objectives. Start slowly by accomplishing your daily tasks, and when you reach the end of the month, assess to see if you have progressed toward your monthly goal through accomplishing your daily tasks. If you haven't, that is completely fine, look back on your daily objectives and see if there's anything you can change or refine to achieve next month's goal. If you prefer, this also works in a weekly format. Use your Sunday as a weekly reset, time to reflect your past week, and also to plan the upcoming week.

5. Stay organized.

Have you ever noticed that when your surroundings are cluttered, it makes it very hard to be comfortable and therefore leads you to be unfocused and distracted? Naturally, humans don't like living in a dirty and messy environment. For you to achieve your goals and accomplish self-discipline, you need to remain organized in either the digital landscape or the world around us. This organizational aptitude also needs to become an incorporated habit into your personal life and professional life. Organizing your life includes the physical act of organizing the things you have within your environment, and also the mental act of consolidating the things in your mind.

By living an organized life, you are living a disciplined life. If you are someone who is constantly scattered and disorganized, start small with your organizational adjustments. Just pick one small space each day for yourself to organize. This space can be just one drawer in your kitchen, the things lying around on your desk, or just straightening out the things on your coffee table. The next day, pick something else to organize like your bathroom drawers or the clothes in your closet. You will begin to notice when clutter builds up, and by having a habit of organization, you will immediately organize things as you use them, so you don't have to spend time organizing it later on.

By decluttering your home or your working environment, you will have plenty of different areas where you can sit down and work on your own goals without interference. Has your home ever been so cluttered that when you do have the motivation to start working on something, you simply don't have the space to do it? To avoid this, keep your home or office clean and organized at all times so that when you have a rush of motivation, you can find a workspace that is clean and ready for you to work undistracted.

Similar to other habits, the habit of organizing yourself can be learned and improved over time. It does require your attention and effort, but it is something that you will reap many benefits from. When you live in a physical space that is organized and clean, your mind will automatically become more stress-free, tranquil, and result in a heightened ability to focus. In turn, by becoming more organized, you are increasing your capacity to be more self-disciplined. Begin to incorporate the good habit of putting things back where they belong after you finish using them instead of just leaving them lying around. Small and insignificant things like this, that we can do daily, heavily impact our quality of life. Give more time and attention to the little things, and you'll begin to see immeasurable benefits.

6. Productive time management.

In this busy world that we live in today, time management is extremely vital if you intend to tick everything off your to do list. An average person works 40 hours a week, unfortunately not including the time that it takes to commute to work, and they will still have to make time for things like exercise, relationships, socializing, family, and achieving the goals they have set. Without effective time management, it will be nearly impossible for you to complete all that you set out to do.

It is important to understand how to properly manage your time, and to stick to your daily or weekly objectives. Mainly, you must prioritize the activities that you need to complete to achieve the larger goals that you have set. If you struggle with time management, and cannot even get the most urgent matters in order, it will severely effect your long term goals that don't require your immediate urgency.

To effectively measure if certain tasks are urgent, important, insignificant, or low priority, you need to take a moment to consider about whether or not the action is beneficial or not. The objectives that fall into the 'low-priority and insignificant' category are known as time-wasters. This category includes things like browsing social media on your phone or binge-watching your favorite Netflix series. Tasks that fall into the category of 'not urgent but important' are likely the short-term goals you have set for yourself. Although you don't need to complete them urgently, they are still important for your self-growth such as exercise or learning new skills. Tasks that are both 'urgent and important' are likely deadlines, or any responsibilities that you have to complete for work.

Your ability to increase productivity comes from your ability to manage your time correctly. Some of the world's most successful individuals are amazing time managers. Everybody has the same 24 hours in a day; we shouldn't use this time wastefully. Start managing your time by categorizing what you need to do throughout the day with the categories I listed above. First, complete the urgent and important tasks, then shift on to the objectives that are less urgent, but still hold significance. Leave the remaining responsibilities that are both low-priority or unimportant until you have completed all your higher priority tasks. This way, you are maximizing your time toward the more important and rewarding objectives.

7. Be persistent.

Persistence is a habit that keeps us from quitting, even when faced with failure. Persistence is what helps us get back up on our feet and continue pushing toward success. You might be wondering why that is. The answer is because achieving high productivity is not an easy skill to obtain. It is really tough. Becoming discouraged or distracted is easy and something that happens to everyone along their journey. Quitting to acquire instant gratification takes far less energy and effort than continuing to push through adversity. However, if you really are chasing success, the hardship required to achieve any goal is simply something that you have to persevere through, no matter what. We must understand that all the successful people in the world have failed numerous times repeatedly. Failure is simply a part of life, and rather than avoiding it and not pursuing your dreams at all in fear of failure, we should learn to persevere and push through.

There are many pathways that you can navigate to instill perseverance as a habit, but the best and most effective is to develop the reasoning as to why you may desire to do the things in life that you're aiming for. If the intentions behind your goals are strong enough, nothing will stand in your way.

8. Improving your sleeping cycle.

When you don't get enough sleep, your brain spends most of its energy focusing on supporting your basic biological functions. This process does not leave much energy for you to spend on exerting your willpower, practicing self-discipline, or driving productivity. Obtaining an appropriate and healthy amount of sleep is a vital requirement for accomplishing anything at a high level. Without enough sleep, your ability to focus begins to lack along with your, judgment, mood, overall health, and diet.

Many research studies have found evidence that people who do not receive a healthy amount of sleep regularly have a greater risk of developing particular diseases. A lack of sleep also has a significantly negative impact on your immune system. This sleep deficiency can also cause you to become sick more frequently, further hindering your ability to effectively achieve your daily goals.

For an adult, a healthy amount of sleep should range between seven to nine hours every night. If you struggle with tracking a quality sleep, avoid eating or drinking anything that contains caffeine at least 5 hours before bedtime so that it doesn't affect your natural sleep cycle. Make a note to avoid ingesting too many toxins during the day, such as cigarettes, alcohol, drugs, or prescription medicine, if you can avoid it.

The benefits of receiving enough sleep are extraordinary, and often overlooked. Aside from the fact that getting enough sleep can help you stay focused and be more productive, it also helps you curb inflammation and pain, lower stress, improve your memory, increase your creativity, sharpen your attention, improve your grades, limit your chances of accidents, and help in eluding depression.

Chapter 3:

Keeping Your Mind Clear

To maximize productivity, the ability to keep your mind clear and in the present is crucial. If you are constantly overcrowding your mind thinking a million thoughts per minute, it will be very difficult for you to focus on the task at hand. In this chapter, I will teach you how to use mindfulness as a technique to increase your productivity. Also, I will teach you a strategy to help make tasks more manageable. Let's dive right in.

Using Mindfulness To Keep You Focused In The Present

Mindfulness meditation is a form of mental training practice that focuses your mind on your thoughts and sensations in the present moment. These thoughts and feelings include your current emotions, physical sensations, and passing judgements. Mindfulness meditation usually involves a breathing practice, mental imagery, awareness of your mind and body, and muscle and body relaxation. It is typically recommended for beginners to follow a guided meditation directing them throughout the whole progression. Without guidance it can be extremely easy to drift away or fall asleep while in a state of meditation. Once you become more skilled in mindfulness meditation, you can perform it without a vocal guide. Start off simple and build on it as you go.

Mindfulness holds many positive benefits and can also help to improve your attention span. Have you ever noticed that you are unable to focus on something for an extended amount of time? A common example would be starting to watch a new television show. You may find yourself drifting off after the first two minutes of a new show and end up doing something out of bad habit like scrolling on your phone with the TV playing in the background. This distraction is all due to having a short attention span. Mindfulness meditation combats this issue. Think of this type of meditation as a form of lifting weights in the gym, but for your attention span.

Let's talk a little about how we can implement mindfulness into your work productivity. We have all experienced the feeling of becoming overwhelmed and scattered at work. This reaction may be caused by an overload of projects or a sense of demotivation to complete current assignments. Did you know that motivation in the workplace has a close relation to mindfulness? Our ability to stay focused and mindful at work is a way to reprogram our minds to think healthier and prevent stress. Below are some benefits to how mindful working can improve your everyday life.

First off, mindfulness in the workplace helps with stress reduction. Stress is a dominant cause of employee disengagement. The European Agency for Safety and Health at Work conducted a study that found that more than half of the 550 million work days that are lost every year from absenteeism are stress-related. Also, 80% of employees report that they feel stress from their workplace and need help learning how to manage it. Some forward-thinking companies nowadays, such as

Google and Adobe, all have mindfulness programs incorporated into the workplace to promote stress reduction in employees. However, if you already practice meditation, you don't need to worry if your workplace doesn't offer a program like this. You can do it yourself.

Mindfulness in the workplace also leads to higher absorption of new information. Allowing your brain to take a break from developing new skills, critical thinking, and problem-solving helps increase learning and creativity. Not encouraging enough breaks and moments to recompose altogether leads to increased tiredness, stress, and thinking blocks. These effects are especially true for those who work in jobs that require an extended period of focus.

Adaptability is a skill that can increase when you are mindful at work. Being able to adapt quickly and efficiently is imperative in a working environment. Did you know that most employers value resourcefulness and adaptability more than they value hard skills? Hard skills include things like coding or programming. Adaptability means that you can quickly adjust accordingly to new situations and handle multiple requests at any given moment. The more you expose yourself to different ways of tackling tasks, learning, and gaining confidence in moments of uncertainty, the more adaptable you will become. Adaptability is one of the most important characteristics of excellent leadership performance. It's typically present in leaders who can manage changing priorities and are comfortable adjusting their perceptions and beliefs.

Problem-solving abilities are also enhanced when you are mindfully working. Problem-solving is the ability to remove chaos from the untrained mind. Removing that clutter leads to better concentration, which ultimately leads to untying the complicated knot of problem-solving. Additionally, mindfulness helps with problem-solving by freeing you from distractions and giving you a new angle to attack from. When you are in the heart of a challenge, try to practice mindfulness. You may be surprised at the increased ability to process information in different ways that will help you to find a resolution.

Being mindful also helps facilitate creativity. The fundamental aspect of creativity is divergent thinking. Divergent thinking refers to the ability to come up with ideas that are outside the box. By practicing mindfulness, you may enhance your creative capacity, allowing you to think more innovatively. Mindfulness frees your mind from distractions, which heightens your ability to look at things around you from a new perspective.

You can strengthen your vitality in the workplace by working mindfully. By definition, vitality means 'exuberant physical strength of mental vigor.' Every single day you commute to work with a certain amount of energy. Some days if you've had a healthy sleep, you may hold a high level of energy. Although, other days if you have had a rough night's sleep, you may feel drained; like you're running on an empty gas tank. Continuing to stay focused and mindful is proven to affect your vitality as it helps you remain positive and focused on your goals and dreams. When your aspirations are clear to you, you are more likely to work towards them with higher vitality.

You might notice that you have an increased level of empathy towards others. We have all heard the saying "to stand in someone else's shoes." Empathy plays a huge role when understanding the minds of other people and relating emotionally to others. Practicing mindfulness at work enables us to have the room in our brain that we require to express empathy for other people.

Mindfulness Meditation Guide

With your new knowledge of how mindfulness can help your productivity in a professional environment, let's learn how to practice mindfulness meditation. The standardized program for this is called the Mindfulness-Based Stress Reduction (MSBR) program. This particular program focuses on your awareness and bringing your attention to the present. This method has been increasingly incorporated into medical settings to treat many health conditions, including stress, pain, and insomnia. It is fairly straight forward; however, having a teacher, guide or program can help navigate you at the beginning for the highest chance of success. Most people meditate for at least ten minutes a day, but even a couple minutes can make an astonishing difference in your well-being. The following technique is a basic technique that will help you get started:

1. Find a quiet place that you feel comfortable in—ideally, your home, office, or somewhere you feel safe. Sit in a chair or on the floor. Ensure that your head and back are upright and straight, but remain in a relaxed position. Lying down is okay too, do what feels comfortable in the environment you are in.
2. Try to sort your thoughts and put aside those that are of the past and future. Stick to the thoughts relating to the present.
3. Direct your awareness to your breath. Focus on the feeling and sensation of air moving through your body as you inhale and again as you exhale. Notice the way your belly inflates and then collapses. Feel the air enter through your nostrils and leave through your mouth. Pay attention to the variances in each breath.
4. Imagine every thought as it comes and goes. Act as if you are watching the clouds, letting them pass by you as you watch each one. Whether your thought is a worry, fear, anxiety, or hope - when these thoughts come up, don't ignore them or try to suppress them. Simply acknowledge them, remain calm, and anchor yourself to your breathing.
5. You may find yourself drifting away in your thoughts. If this happens, observe where your mind went off to, and without making a judgment, simply return to your breathing. Keep in mind that this happens a lot with beginners; try not to be too hard on yourself when this happens. Always use your breathing as an anchor again.
6. As we near the end of the 10-minute session, sit for a minute or two, and become aware of where you physically are before returning back to your day ahead.

To further your mindfulness meditation practice, I have provided you with an additional example of a mindfulness technique that you can use on your own.

This mindfulness technique helps to combat anxiety and stress that can occur when you are not breathing correctly. Have you ever noticed that you breath is heavily effected when you find yourself in a stressful situation? This exercise will help you evade unhealthy breathing habits that can lead to a decline in physical and psychological health, leading to decreased productivity. Interestingly, this type of meditation is quite a large part of yoga culture and tradition.

Breath Awareness in Meditation:

1. Begin by sitting in a comfortable place with your back straight on a chair, bench, or even a cushion. Close your eyes and rest your body for a few moments. Try to soften the sides of your rib cage along with your abdominal wall. Doing so will allow your breath to flow deeper. You will begin to notice a cleansing sensation when you exhale and a feeling of nourishment when you inhale. Be patient, and allow the relaxed movement of your inhale and exhale to become smooth. It will likely take several minutes for you to sense that it is quite effortless. When you have achieved this, you are ready to continue to the next step.

2. Next, relax your body, beginning from your head down to your toes. Feel the sensation of relaxation flow from your toes back to your head. Start to slowly move your attention through the body, releasing tensions just like the widespread body scan technique. When you finish, return to the top of your head and sense your entire body as a whole. Breathe as if your whole body is taking a breath. Let yourself follow the effortlessness of your breath. As time goes by, continue to monitor your breath.

3. Bring your awareness to the touch of the air in the nostrils. Start to transition from breathing with your whole body to breathing

in with your nostrils. Allow it to feel natural and comfortable, and give yourself a few minutes to do this. Remember to bring your attention back to your breathing if your mind starts to wander off at any moment. Throughout your practice sessions, train yourself to maintain your focus and try not to break your awareness or breathing. Your mind won't stop thinking, so don't expect that it will. Instead, just maintain breath awareness.

4. When thoughts arise in your mind, let it come and go. Do not focus your attention and awareness on your passing thoughts, but do not turn them into your enemy either. Just simply, let them float by you like a cloud. As you continue through this exercise, your breath awareness will deepen. It will slowly become profoundly relaxing, and you will begin to notice changes in the state of your body and mind. These subtle changes are critical checkpoints to your concentration and signal that your breath awareness meditation has nearly completed its inner work.

Starting Your Tasks

Although mindfulness can help you increase focus and improve your attention span, you must actually start your tasks in the first place for this to take full effect. Let's talk about a couple of varying strategies you can implement to ensure that you get a start on your tasks.

- **Strategy #1: The Swiss Cheese Method**

People often believe in this strange myth that they need a huge chunk of uninterrupted time to accomplish whatever they are looking to accomplish. However, if you don't have a large chunk of time dedicated to work on your task, such as that report that is due in two weeks, you are making a mistake by delaying it until you find yourself with a few hours of uninterrupted time. Rather than repeatedly putting it off, you should try to apply a technique called the "Swiss Cheese Approach." Swiss cheese is a type of cheese that is famed for its numerous holes.

The Swiss Cheese Approach involves the following elements:

- Working in small 'holes' of time. Set out to complete some work in just 15, 20, or 30 minutes.
- Work away at large tasks by poking small 'holes' consistently.

This approach is efficient because of these reasons:

- Once you start working on a task, it no longer feels as overwhelming or difficult as before to begin.
- By poking small 'holes' in a task, you'll make little but constant progress.
- This approach will help you build a sense of 'forward momentum'; you are motivated to keep doing more once you start.
- Each time you complete a small portion of the task, it will give you a sense of accomplishment.
- You are making good use of small portions of time rather than wasting it completely.

The next time you find yourself with only 15 – 20 minutes to work on your task/project, rather than telling yourself that you don't have enough time, or waiting until you have a longer time block, ask yourself these questions below:

- "Is there a small 'hole' in this project that I can start with?"
- "How can I use this time to poke a small 'hole' in my task?"
- "What can I get done in 10 – 15 minutes?"

By continuing to poke 'holes' into your tasks and projects whenever you find yourself with some time to spare, you will be surprised to find that you have accomplished a lot.

- **Strategy #2: Breaking Down Large Tasks Into Smaller Ones**

One main reason you may suffer from low productivity is finding that the work you need to complete is too overwhelming. Start by just breaking down whatever that task is into smaller objectives and then focus on ticking off one at a time. If you find yourself still wanting to procrastinate after you've already broken it down, then break it down even more. You will eventually get to a point where the task you need to do is so easy that you would feel very badly about yourself if you avoided it.

For example, imagine that one of your goals is to manage your money better. It is tax season, and you need to complete your taxes to understand your financial situation. Imagine that you are feeling overwhelmed as you don't even know where to begin in filing taxes. You are also afraid that you may owe money to the government that you might not have. Here is how I would break down the large and broad task of 'filing taxes':

1. Research the best way to file taxes for beginners
2. Explore my options (either downloading software for DIY or going to a tax filing company/agency)
3. Pick which option suits you best.
4. Gather the documents that are suggested based on which option you chose in step #2
5. Follow the instructions given to you by the tax software or the tax professional.

Suddenly that one large task of 'filing taxes' became much more manageable. Instead of thinking about filing taxes as one large unit, you are now starting with a simple google search of the best way to file taxes for beginners. From there, now you can make an educated decision on which method is easiest for you to proceed with. By taking things one step at a time, your mind becomes less overwhelmed.

Chapter 4:

Productivity Strategies

There are various strategies that will help you improve productivity and minimize procrastination. These approaches are all simple but effective,. However, you may need to figure out which approach will work best for you. Identifying the most effective strategies for your working style is crucial in improving your productivity in the long run.

Removing Your Distractions And Temptations

In this day and age, our homes and workspaces are filled with endless amounts of digital distractions. Is it possible to get rid of all of them? No. The reality is that we rely so much on technology that the same equipment that helps us become more productive and effective is also the same equipment that brings us endless distractions. If possible, you should turn off your smartphone or mute notifications, and put away other temptations like video games that can cause you to get sidetracked.

Everyone has their own poison or set of distractions/weaknesses, and it can range from small things like an unhealthy snack to something that hinders your productivity, like playing a video game for hours on end. By understanding your weaknesses, you can make accommodations for yourself that will help remove some of those temptations.

For instance, if you were looking to lose weight and get fit, but knew that your weakness was that you always ate chocolate ice cream after dinner every night. Your first priority would be to remove that temptation. Next time you're out food shopping, avoid that sneaky chocolate ice cream at the checkout. By not having chocolate in the home, you'd be unable to fall into the temptation of indulging, which will hinder your wonderful progress in the gym. However, this does not mean that you will never be able to eat chocolate ice cream again. This measure simply means that you should preferably indulge in your favorite treats when you have achieved a certain portion of your goal. Use this system of rewarding yourself to congratulate your effort and hard work. Remember, rewarding oneself is important to self-discipline, as well.

The first thing you need to do is find out what your weaknesses and distractions are. Are you a chronic phone-scroller? Or do you like to snack during inappropriate times? Depending on what your goals are, remove those temptations where possible. For someone trying to stay on a healthy diet, get rid of literally every piece of junk food in your house so that you cannot be tempted. If you need to complete a work report, disconnect your television, video games, and turn off your smartphone until you finish the necessary tasks. An alternative idea could be to find a work environment that is far from these distractions, perhaps taking your laptop to a bench in the park or the library. If these options aren't available, delay instant gratification for as long as you can.

Reward System

Like anything else in life, it is necessary to give yourself a break and reward yourself. Give yourself something to look forward to by planning an appropriate reward when you accomplish your goals. This concept is not much different from when you were a little kid, and you got a treat from your parents for showing good behavior. When a person has something to look forward to, it gives them the extra motivation needed to succeed.

Do you like chocolate chip cookies? Then give yourself a cookie when you finish with your tasks. Do you enjoy playing video games? Then allow yourself to play two hours of video games once you finish with your work. What about a glass of wine? Do you like wine? Let yourself have a glass of wine when you finish your work.

Anticipation is a powerful thing. It gives you something to focus on so that you are not left thinking merely of all the things you need to change. When you have achieved one of your goals, you can find yourself a new goal and a new means to keep motivating yourself to progress forward. However, the reward should not be detrimental for you. For example, if you are trying to lower your alcohol intake, your reward for not drinking as often as you did before should not be that you will binge drink next Friday. The last thing you want is to derail your prior efforts by reverting back to your old habits.

The Pomodoro Technique

The Pomodoro technique is a method that was invented by Frances Cocirillo in the 1980s that helps people manage their time better, making them more productive, focused, and shrewder. For lots of people, their enemy is time. People are constantly racing against the clock to complete projects or meet deadlines. The Pomodoro method teaches you to work *with* time rather than battling against it using a timer to break down work into intervals, separated by short breaks in between. The idea behind this technique is that the timer instills a sense of urgency, rather than feeling like you have an endless amount of time to complete your tasks. The Pomodoro Technique is comprised of five easy steps:

1. Identify a task list that you want to complete.

The tasks could be anything. It could be a large task like remodeling your bathroom or a small undertaking such as cleaning out your kitchen cabinets. It doesn't matter what task you choose as long as it is deserving of your undivided attention.

2. Set a timer for 25 minutes.

The next step is to make a promise to yourself. Tell yourself that you will spend 25 minutes on this task and that you will not interrupt yourself. That sounds easy enough, right? After all, 25 minutes is a very short amount of time.

3. Work on your set task until the timer rings.

Fully immerse yourself into that set task for 25 minutes. If something else comes to mind that you realize that you have to do, make a mental note to do it at a later time. This allocated time block is set for your dedicated task alone.

4. Take a short 5 minute break.

You've done well! Now, it's time for you to take a short break. This break can include whatever you like. Do you want to meditate? Do you want to make a cup of coffee? Do you want to sit down and rest for a little while? Whatever it may be, now is the time to do it. Your mind and body will thank you later.

5. Rinse and repeat.

This process should be repeated four times to complete a Pomodoro cycle. Once you have finished working through four-timer rings, or what we call "Pomodoro's," you can give yourself a longer break. 20 –

30 minutes is a good amount of time for a break. During this time, your brain will assimilate new information and take a rest before the next round of Pomodoro. Just keep repeating this process throughout the day if required.

Two-Minute Rule & Motivation

Some people use the excuse that they "don't have enough time to do this right now." However, there is a huge flaw in this outlook. There will always be time to work on something; you just have to review your priorities.

The two-minute rule caters to those attempting to build new habits. More often than not any new habit can be scaled down into a two minute version. For example, 'reading before bed each night' becomes 'reading one or two pages.' 'Learning the piano' becomes practicing the 'C Mixolydian Mode' for two minutes. The idea behind this strategy is to remove all of the excuses for starting. There's no way out. Who doesn't have two minutes spare to quickly practice their new habit. A great bonus to this is once you have started a task it's so much easier to continue on with the project. Have you ever dreaded starting a project only to find that once you started you worked for hours on end? Crazy right? It's all about repetition and drilling the idea of just starting into your thinking process. If you keep on working then great, that was our goal. If you don't that's okay, you can always try again later. Overtime it will only get easier and easier. The goal is to just simply start.

You may often put off doing certain tasks until you're "in the mood" or 'feeling inspired.' By telling yourself that you are waiting for a certain burst of motivation is merely procrastination in disguise. Rather than waiting for a sense of inspiration to come before getting started on your task/work, you need to tell yourself firmly that this work needs to be done regardless of how much or how little inspiration you feel. By doing this, you will find that inspiration becomes a product of discipline. When you begin working on the task you've set, you will start feeling fulfilled, leading to a boost of genuine inspiration. Simply just stop wasting time waiting for the feeling of inspiration to hit you. Just like Picasso once said, "Inspiration exists, but it has to find you working."

Another excuse is that you may be 'too tired' or 'too stressed" to perform certain tasks. This is singlehandedly the most common excuse used in the world of procrastination. If you find yourself in a negative mood, all you will want to do is stop working and find instant gratification in any shape or form. This other activity could be just sitting at home relaxing, indulging in a snack, or going out for a beer. You might then rationalize that you would complete your work faster and be more productive if you re-attempted it at a later time when you felt better. There are two important aspects to note here. First of all, it is impossible to tell what kind of mood you will be in the future. For all we know, you could be in the same mood tomorrow and fall into the same excuse in some sort of unproductive loop. Secondly, this is not a common thought, but working through a hard task can actually enhance your mood. The feeling of achievement and satisfaction that comes with finishing a task, no matter how pleasant or unpleasant, often lifts you out of a bad mood. Especially if you can get a reward afterwards.

Believe it or not, motivation comes when you take action. It doesn't just appear. If it did, everyone would be able to complete their work, and procrastination wouldn't even exist. People often have the wrong mindset where they think that they need to feel completely motivated before they start working on a task/job. This mindset is unrealistic. When you see progress, you start to see the fruits to your labor, and you become motivated to keep working until you can enjoy that "fruit". You might be wondering, what about the motivation that is needed to start working altogether? The answer to this is that you need to understand WHY you are doing a job. Before you even begin working on it, you should know what the benefits are going to be. This is often where you may gain some initial motivation as you can envision the end goal of performing this particular task.

By understanding the benefits of completing a task or job, you can fully estimate its importance. Moreover, you should be utilizing prioritization to get the most urgent and important work out of the way first. In regards to smaller tasks/jobs, simply understanding the benefits of completing that task should be enough motivation. For larger tasks and jobs, you must have a way to measure your progress to gain motivation and confidence from your work as you go.

Time Blocking

This technique is another simple one that works wonders – block off your time in the calendar. Write down EVERYTHING into your calendar. Whether it's conference calls, meetings, or even happy hour drinks with your friends – write it in. Once events or tasks are in your calendar, there should be little room for excuses as to why you can't do it; you have allowed the time for it. Schedule in things like exercise, your afternoon snack, and even a 15-minute break – this will help you break up your day to keep you sharp for other tasks. It might seem tedious at first but entering in everything you can think of allows for a complete insight into how your day will play out.

Filling your calendar is crucial as it forces you to complete every task; otherwise, all of your other tasks become compromised. If you procrastinate and don't stay on schedule, fun and leisurely events that you have scheduled on your calendar will get pushed further and further back until you may no longer have the time to enjoy those occasions. Having a filled up calendar will help you avoid using the excuse of "I will do it tomorrow." An old saying goes, "never put off till tomorrow what you can do today." Instead of resisting temptation, try to think of it in a way where you're doing yourself a favor. By planning out your calendar a few days in advance, you KNOW that you have the time to do a task today and that it can't wait until tomorrow because guess what, you have fully booked that day too!

Play A Game Using Your To-Do List

For those who procrastinate a lot, this technique will help make beating procrastination a fun experience. You can do this in many ways; the most popular method is to set a point system for yourself. Write out a list of tasks you have to do in your day and associate one point to each of those tasks. State a few rewards that will cost a certain amount of points. For instance; 1-hour of video games tonight – 3 points and ordering takeout from your favorite restaurant 6 points. Every time you complete a task on your to-do list, you gain one point. You can then trade in your points for a prize of your choosing.

If you cannot hold yourself accountable for this technique, it is good to get someone else involved. Ask your roommate, your significant other or a family member to audit how many points you have and make sure you don't accept a prize when you don't have enough points. This exercise makes completing tasks fun, and if you have a competitive nature, you will probably smash out way more tasks than you needed to on that list.

Goal Setting

A huge part of improving productivity is to ensure that you are not losing sight of your goals. Make sure to clearly define your goals and figure out what is most important to you. You can do this by practicing the technique of active goal setting. As we have previously discussed, active goal setting differs greatly from passive goal-setting. Passive goal setting means that you are setting goals that lack detail and planning. This makes it hard for you to keep track of your progress and know what still needs to be done to achieve that goal. Active goal setting is the complete opposite. Active goal setting is the act writing out these goals and making sure that they have an important and definitive meaning. It's crucial that these goals remain measurable and very specific. To successfully have an active goal, you have to define a pathway to achieve it. So take your long-term goals, reverse engineer a pathway to that goal, and engage in the smaller daily objectives to achieve that bigger goal.

If you haven't already, grab a pen and start writing down your goals!

Outsourcing Tasks

Typically, if you face something you don't want to do, you are more likely to procrastinate, and experience lowered productivity levels. If this is a common occurrence, see if you can avoid this task by either delegating it, automating it, or eliminating it completely. Here are some tips to try out:

- Check to see if you really need to complete this task
- Ask yourself if there is someone else who is much better suited to completing this task. If possible, you may be able to swap it or delegate it (e.g., if someone else likes that job more, you could potentially offer a trade with that person for a job of theirs that you might like better)
- If your tolerance for frustration is low, try to break down this job into smaller pieces and complete them one at a time
- If your tolerance for frustration is higher, you can schedule a block of time where you take away all distractions and just do this task until you finish it.

If you outsource a job/task remember that you will likely find more success if you assign this specific task to someone you know will enjoy it. By choosing someone with an interest in that task, they will complete the job in a much faster fashion and at a higher standard.

The 80-20 Rule

When it comes to productivity, a rule of thumb is that you should always complete the most important tasks first. A good system you may want to try is the 80-20 rule. The 80-20 rule is also known as the Pareto Principle. This rule is based around the idea that 80% of outcomes result from 20% of all inputs and causes in any given event. Imagine the difference tweaking the 80% by delegating or eliminating unimportant tasks allowing more time for the 20%. Think about how much impact that could have on your business, workouts, or life.

Here is an example of the 80/20 rule in action. An acquaintance of mine was looking to boost his sales in a commission based business model. Upon analyzing his profit margins he realized that 20% of his client base contributed to 80% of his profits. However, he spent the same amount of time on low-profit clients as he did high-profit clients. You'd think that sounds a bit off right? My associates first instinct was to kindly, and politely delegate other industry professionals to handle his low-profit client base that he was no longer focused on. His second motion was to rebrand his approach and began combing through his high-profit client base to understand them more as a demographic. With this new found knowledge of his audience he was able to refine his criteria for new clients and increase his income astronomically.

Parkinson's Law

Parkinson's law states that 'work expands to fill the time available for its completion.' This means that if you are allocating a week to complete a three-hour task, then psychologically, you will feel as that task increases in complexity and becomes more daunting so that it fills up a week's worth of time. This task may not even be worth a whole week's worth of time, but just the tension and stress alone about having to get that task done will tire you out. By learning to assign the correct amount of time to complete a task, you will gain back more time, and your task will naturally reduce in complexity.

The point here is that you should be applying Parkinson's law to your specific tasks and deadlines. For instance, if one of your goals were to finish building a shelf, cut the time you think you need in half. If you guessed that it would take you three hours, give yourself one and a half hours to do it. Expand this to the rest of your tasks. Make a list of all the tasks you have to do and divide each task by the amount of time it will take to complete it. Then, give yourself just 50% of that time. Treat this deadline as you would with any other deadline. If you said you would give yourself 30 minutes, don't secretly give yourself an hour. Try to get it done in 30 minutes.

At the beginning of this exercise, you may find yourself figuring out how accurate your time projections are. Some tasks may be spot on while you might have inflated others incredibly. Those tasks that are spot-on for time may be tasks you can't complete faster, so you may need to allow for more time when needed. However, the tasks where you feel like the time is inflated, cut it down by at least half and continue to try to race the clock. Using a digital timer if you are working on the computer will be very helpful in this situation. Using a timer will allow you to see how much time you have left as you are working and instill a sense of urgency. It will also show you second by second how much you are completing and how much time you have left to complete the rest of your tasks.

Conclusion

First off, I'd like to say that you have taken the first and hardest step into this journey of improving your productivity. As you may have learned, it's not easy to gather motivation to get tasks done while overcoming instant gratification, but also not necessary. Because you decided to learn brand new ideas to help you become more productive, you have already taken a huge step in the right direction. You now comprehend numerous factors that affect an individual's productivity, such as; procrastination, habits, and self-control. Understanding the fundamental pillars of productivity will help you improve the most important skills to help you achieve more for yourself.

Consistency is the key here when you are looking to improve on any level. Our daily habits are deep-rooted neural pathways in our brain that become more ingrained over time. If it took you ten years to get into the bad habit of no exercising, it'd likely take a decent effort or push to pull you out of that rut. Although that sounds daunting at first, I promise you it will get easier the more consistent you are with it. Developing healthy habits is just the same. By remaining consistent with your mindfulness and exercising the many techniques that you have picked up, you will retrain your way of thinking. Once your healthy habits are deeply rooted, you won't even have to think about it anymore. That's the level that you want to obtain. Automation.

Not every productivity technique works perfectly for everyone. Some individuals may find certain techniques extremely effective, but others may find those same techniques not as useful. Figure out which techniques work best with you and utilize those to combat your procrastination. Everybody is different; trial and error is the key here. Keep in mind that these techniques require several weeks of practice and repetition to be effective. Don't expect to just switch techniques if you don't see progress after a few days. Give each one some time to imbed into your neural pathways.

One important thing that I want to note before ending this off is that everyone has lapses and relapses when altering their mental structure. Alike to those battling anxiety, depression, or self-esteem, individuals battling with low levels of productivity may sometimes relapse into their bad habits. This is completely okay. The point here is that you forgive yourself, and you continue practicing the techniques. Just because you have relapsed once, twice, or ten times does not mean you have failed. There is no failure here. So if one day you decide to binge-watch your favorite Netflix series rather than working on a paper that's due in a week, that is okay. You may feel guilt at that present moment, but it does not mean you should give up on the process entirely. Simply accept the fact that you had a lapse, figure out what you did wrong at that moment, and apply it to your future growth. Keep your head up and remain consistent. The only thing in your way is yourself, so stop procrastinating and get it done!

www.ingramcontent.com/pod-product-compliance
Lightning Source LLC
Chambersburg PA
CBHW071758080526
44588CB00013B/2286